→ 52
TIMESAVERS
FOR
ON·THE·GO
MOMS

52 TIMESAVERS FOR ON·THE·GO MOMS

Kate Redd

OLIVER NELSON

THOMAS NELSON PUBLISHERS
Nashville

Published in Nashville, Tennessee, by Oliver-Nelson Books, a division of Thomas Nelson, Inc.

The Bible version used in this publication is THE NEW KING JAMES VERSION. Copyright © 1979, 1980, 1982, Thomas Nelson, Inc., Publishers.

Printed in the United States of America.

Library of Congress Cataloging-in-Publication Data

Redd, Kate.
   52 timesavers for on-the-go-moms / Kate Redd.
     p.   cm.
   ISBN 0-8407-9652-8 (pbk.)
   1. Working mothers—United States—Time management.
2. Mothers—United States—Time management.   I. Title.
II. Title: Fifty-two timesavers for on-the-go moms.
HQ759.48.R43   1993
640′.43′0852—dc20   92-45062
                                                      CIP

3   4   5   6 — 98   97   96   95   94   93

To

my mother,
Catherine,

who gracefully balanced career and home,
and to her friends

Becky	Helen
Enid	Grace
Annie	Dorothy
Jeanne	Marge

who were also "working moms"

◑ Contents

◑ Introduction

I've never met a mother who didn't work—hard. I've never met a mother who wasn't busy—sometimes overly.

This book has been written especially for those mothers who feel as if their lives are "overstuffed" to the point where something needs to give or something (or someone) will break.

Three assumptions are made in offering these suggestions to you:

Assumption #1—*You* can *take charge of many of the details of your life, and if you take charge of some of the details, the big picture will seem clearer and more do-able.*

Many women may feel as if they can't change the major facts of their lives. They *need* to work. They *have* children. They *must* do their best. They *get* precious little help. They *never* have enough time for everything they feel they must do, much less what they want to do. The result is that most women feel overwhelmed in today's world— at the *macro* level.

Most women, however, will admit that they *can* make certain decisions about the style of their homes, clothes, and personal appearance, their daily schedules, and the noise level in their homes. The good news is that women do have a great deal of power over their worlds—at the *micro* level. This book offers suggestions aimed at this level.

Assumption #2—*The one thing that most women wish they had was more time.*

Often, a mother's desire is to spend more time with her children. Or, to have more time alone to focus her thoughts, muster her energy, relax, and clear her heart and mind of a day's stresses.

This book offers suggestions for squeezing more personal and relational time out of a day. Again, at the micro level. Minutes here. Minutes there. Quality-time niches in a full schedule.

Assumption #3—*Nobody can do it all or be it all.* At least not simultaneously.

Once a woman accepts that fact, she usually finds it easier to relax into her present set of circumstances and to make the most of them. The key is "balance"—developing a mix of commitments and responsibilities that is not only possible, but rewarding. This book offers suggestions from that perspective.

Some things can't be cut short. Whereas tasks have shortcuts, relationships don't. They take time. They require effort. This book can help you find faster, more efficient ways to accomplish tasks and reduce the stress associated with having too many tasks to do in too little time. It does not attempt to offer suggestions, however, for finding simpler ways to love. Indeed, there are no shortcuts. Our children require our time, our attention, our praise, our training, our affection. My hope is that as you streamline your tasks and duties, you'll find yourself expanding your relationship with those who matter most —your family.

1 🕐 One Calendar

Keep only one calendar on which you list your personal, family, and work commitments and appointments.

Nothing can cause confusion faster than having one calendar at home and another at work, or having multiple calendars within a home.

Find one format—daily, weekly, or monthly—and stick with it. Otherwise, you may forget to transfer something from your monthly calendar to your daily schedule.

Find a version that you can carry with you. Consider purchasing one of the highly compact "systems" presently on the market, in which you can mix and match several types of information sheets that are readily interchangeable and replaceable. As a base, you probably will want to have a calendar, an address and phone listing, and blank sheets for making notes. Then consider adding other specialty sheets.

Limit the number of people who can add items to your schedule. At work, your secretary may need access to your calendar to make appointments or schedule meetings on your behalf. Be sure you develop a means of communication so you know what has been added and when.

Apply the same principle at home. Try using a "calendar bulletin board." Notices from school, hand scribbled notes, and so forth are pinned to the board by all members of the family. If an event is immediate, family members write the message boldly and put it in a corner of the bulletin board labeled *Now!*

Once a week, the family adds these events to a master calendar—in some cases, making decisions about what they will and will not commit themselves to doing.

Don't feel you have to do it all.   You don't need to accept every invitation or go to every event or meeting. Other things you shouldn't miss, such as parent-teacher conferences and your children's school play. Try weeding out your *possible* time commitments into Must, Not This Time, and Maybe-If-We-Feel-Like-It categories (and then drop most of the maybe items).

Schedule free time and family time.   A calendar can be your best time-management tool for implementing your own personal and family priorities. Mark blocks of time in which you choose *not* to schedule an outside-the-family obligation or event. Set aside at least an hour or two for yourself each week. Regard these appointments with yourself or with your family with the same degree of importance as an appointment with your best client or your most important colleague or associate.

Anticipate upcoming obligations.   For example, if you're scheduled to take cupcakes to your children's school on Thursday, write a note on your calendar for the previous Saturday reminding you to get cupcake ingredients. (Or just write, Buy cupcakes, on Wednesday's list of things to do!)

2 🕐 Order from Catalogs

Shopping by catalogs has a number of advantages:

- No hassle of driving to and from the mall.

- No parking problems.

- No displays of temper from those who may feel they are being "dragged" to the store.

- No waiting in lines for clerks to answer questions about an item or to ring up your sale.

- No pressure from sales personnel. You can evaluate the item in the privacy of your own home.

- Availability of items you may not be able to find in your town. (By catalog, you can even buy Gucci from a desert-isle home.)

- Unlimited "open" hours in most cases. Shop at midnight if you like!

Shopping by catalog allows you to shop virtually anywhere—in the car as you wait for the children to get out of school; during a coffee break at work; or at the dentist's office as you wait for your appointment.

For those who have never shopped by catalog, or who remember only the old days of giant major store catalogs (such as Montgomery Ward or Sears), be encouraged. Catalog shopping now has many features it didn't have in the past.

- Most companies now have easy return policies for items that don't fit or don't meet with your approval. Open with care the packages in which catalog items are sent, so you can use them if you need to return the items. Be sure to read the catalog's return policy before you order.

- Look for size information before ordering. Most catalogs that offer clothing include size charts, and some offer over-the-phone advice.

- Virtually all companies have toll-free numbers for ordering. Just have your credit card handy.

- Prices have never been better. Many discount catalogs are available. Do check, however, the amount charged for shipping and handling.

Perhaps the best word in the catalog world is *variety*. There's a catalog now for just about any type of item you'd like to purchase. A number of children's specialty catalogs are available, too.

How do you get on the mailing lists for quality catalogs? Magazines frequently offer order forms for catalogs. Some catalogs advertise with toll-free numbers. Be assured that once you begin to purchase from catalogs, you are likely to end up on the mailing lists of more catalogs than you can accommodate!

Catalogs are an especially good way to shop for gifts.

Unless you *must* see the item before it is sent to the future bride, graduate, or relative in a distant state, have the item sent directly to the recipient. You'll save time, wrapping hassles, and mailing fees.

3 ● Choose No-Fuss Clothing

Although the frills and crisp collars of a child's garment may look enticing on the rack or the catalog page, don't be seduced. The same goes for rayon jackets and silk skirts. If a garment catches your eye, check the tag that tells you about the care of the garment before you try it on.

Busy schedules don't allow for fussy clothes. Choose garments that

- *Can be washed.* Dry cleaning takes time and money, and invariably, the garment you want is out of commission. Many fabrics that were once automatically labeled dry clean only now have "washability," including washable silks and woolens. Bear in mind that if an item can't be washed, a spill or spot probably can't be cleaned easily. That means you also have to deal with stain control. It's simpler to buy garments that can be washed, and which

- *Don't need to be ironed.* If your husband's shirts or your blouses must be ironed, consider letting a laundry service do them. Many items don't need pressing if you take them from the dryer as soon as they are dry.

- *Have few buttons, snaps, or other closures.* If you buy a garment with buttons, take a few minutes before the first wearing to reinforce the stitching on any loose buttons. You'll save yourself the frustration of trying to match lost buttons later. Many garments come with extra buttons. If that's the case, be sure to label any little bags in which the extra buttons are packaged with a brief description of the garment to which it belongs, and put both button and bag in your button jar. (Don't have a button jar? You can create one from a clean peanut butter or mayonnaise jar.)

- *Fit loosely.* Tight garments result in ripped seams and difficult-to-fix tears, not to mention lack of comfort. Most children appreciate loose-fitting garments, and the more active you are, the more you'll appreciate garments that don't pinch or limit your mobility.

- *Are made of printed or plaid fabrics.* They hide little spills, spots, and stains far better than solid fabrics.

- *Are wrinkle resistant.* Knits are wonderful for busy moms. They not only stretch in all the ways you need to stretch, but they resist wrinkles.

Develop a mix-'n'-match wardrobe.   Build a wardrobe of classic designs in which you can combine lots of pieces in different ways to create new looks. Think layered. A couple of easy-care knit skirts with a variety of no-iron colored T-shirts, a couple of cardigans or pullover sweaters, and a blazer or two can make an entire wardrobe that will last for years.

Choose classic styles for your children, too. They pass down from child to child with greater ease.

No-fuss, easy-to-combine garments save you time and decrease the likelihood of hearing the mournful cry, M-o-m, I don't have anything to wear!

4 ● Decompression Time

Consider your own heart and learn a lesson from it. Your heart rests between beats.

Give yourself some "breathers" during your busy day. In fact, the busier the day, the tighter the deadline, the more frantic the atmosphere, the more you need to take quality breaks.

This is especially important as you move from work to home. Don't race pell-mell from office to freeway to driveway to kitchen. Take ten or fifteen minutes to shift gears. Here are some suggestions:

- *Change clothes.* Get comfortable. You'll feel more refreshed and your work clothes will be spared kitchen splatters.

- *Sort the mail or listen to your phone messages.* Catch up with the information of the day.

- *Have a cold beverage and perhaps a nutritious snack.* This takes the edge off hunger pangs and gives you a little more lead time for fixing a proper meal.

- *Sit down.* Put your feet up. You may be surprised at how much more relaxed you feel after just five minutes in that position.

- *Keep the TV off.* This is a time to decompress and to shut down the stimuli of the day. Quiet music may be soothing.

- *Adopt a "being present in the moment" attitude.* Coming home is more than an activity. It's a shift in mind set.

It's especially important for you to be available for conversation during those first few minutes of "coming home" time, no matter who the family member is who's coming home. If you are already home when your children come home from school, make yourself available to them for those first few minutes of at-home time. If it's your husband coming home, pour yourselves soft drinks and relax together for a few minutes. If you're the one coming home, toss everything else aside and curl up with your family for a few minutes.

Listen.

Absorb.

Take in.

Unwind.

There will be plenty of time for giving out as the evening progresses. And those fifteen or so minutes of decompression time will help give you the energy and attitude-adjustment you need to make it gracefully through the remaining hours of the day.

5 ● Time-Outs

Closely akin to decompression time are "time-outs." These are times when you simply need to check out from all obligations, commitments, and availability to others. Time-outs can also be defined as "quality alone time."

Break the mood. Every person needs a little time alone every day. The benefits are invaluable and numerous. Perhaps the most noteworthy benefit is this: a complete break in mood.

If you're angry, a time-out can help you calm down.

If you're stressed out or frustrated, a time-out can help you regroup and refocus.

If you're feeling overwhelmed by a problem or question (or ten dozen questions), a time-out can help you slow down enough to think through an answer.

If you're exhausted, a time-out can be like a mini-vacation, a pause that refreshes.

A "think break." Many parents and teachers use time-outs as a means of discipline, so most children have an understanding of what a time-out is. You can explain your time-out to your children this way: "When I give you a time-out, it's so you can think about what you have done. When Mommy takes a time-out, it's so she can think about what she needs to do." You may want to call your time-out a think break.

You probably have a place where you send your children for a time-out. You need to have a time-out place, too. It might be a favorite chair in a sun room, a den, or a bedroom.

Give yourself at least five minutes, preferably ten. Set a timer that your children can see. The first few times you declare a think break, your children may test the boundaries. Insist that for every interruption or every violation of good behavior during your think break, you will require a minute of time-out time for them! They'll soon get the message that you will be accessible soon—when the buzzer goes off—and that for the present, you are to be left alone.

Escape, mentally.   Once alone, sit or lie down with your feet up.

Breathe deeply and rhythmically.

Close your eyes.

Imagine a faraway setting or a place of beauty. See yourself walking or relaxing there. Imagine the sounds and aromas of that beautiful imaginary place. Imagine as many details as possible about the way the place looks and the way you feel—comfortable, relaxed, barefoot.

Only when you are completely relaxed should you allow your mind to turn to any questions or problems you are facing. You may find that the problem seems less intense, or that you have an answer you didn't have previously. A think break can provide a creative shift of gears, a time for the brain to sort data and come up with solutions or ideas. It also can be a time in which a problem is put into clearer

Daydream a Vacation

Nearly everyone has a dream vacation in mind. Until you are able to travel to your ideal destination, here are some daydream vacations you might take!

- Imagine yourself lounging on a beautiful beach of white sand on a day when the weather is perfect. You have the beach all to yourself—to roam, to build a sand castle, to swim, to gather shells, or to gaze into tidal pools.

- Imagine yourself standing under a waterfall in a beautiful tropical forest, with exotic blossoms and deep green foliage all around the shallow pool you have chosen. The area is free of bugs, snakes, and intruders, so you can splash, dance, or float on the water to your heart's content.

- Imagine you are lying in a beautiful meadow, staring upward at a deep blue sky. See the cloud formations as they pass overhead. Watch the flowers around you sway gently in the breeze.

- Imagine you are in front of a roaring fireplace in a snowbound lodge, curled up on a comfortable sofa with an afghan tucked around you. Your food and water will last for weeks, and you have electricity, a phone, and plenty of your favorite reading material. You can invite anyone you choose to spend a few minutes or hours with you, doing what *you* choose to do!

perspective; very often, problems shrink in size or become less intense.

Think breaks help you to be more present and more relaxed with your children and spouse. They help you feel more in control of your own emotions. Best of all, they are free, and you can take as many as you need in any given day!

6 🕐 Sorting and Storing: Spaces and Skills

Cleaning messy rooms takes time, energy, and often involves confrontations. What can you do?

1) Provide sufficient sorting and storing space for your children's "stuff." That may mean adding shelves or investing in some easy-to-use plastic stacking units. A child will find it easier to create order in a room with ample sorting and storing capacity.

Consider adding a Peg-Board to your children's rooms for hanging rain gear, winter coats, rackets, etc.

2) Teach your children how to cluster items. For example, all the pieces to a puzzle should be kept in a box together, and all puzzles should be stored on one shelf or in one plastic storage bin. The following items can be clustered:

- Clothes
- Underwear
- Shoes
- Books
- Games and puzzles
- Art and craft supplies

- Toys and dolls

- School supplies

- Sporting equipment

If your children have a doll house or a train set, items related to them should also be stored together.

3) Teach your children that "everything has a place, and there's a place for everything." This means items are found quickly, resulting in less frustration for children and mom.

4) Teach your children the "one at a time" rule. This also may be stated as the "use it and return it to its place" rule.

For example, if your child pulls out a tin of Legos, he or she should put them away before pulling out a puzzle. The same rule applies to clothes.

The practice is both sound and do-able because it is based on a well-proven underlying principle: children actually *like* order. Children who use one item at a time and are able to restore it to a place of its own and access it readily along with other like items, feel a greater sense of control over their space and possessions.

Mom benefits.   The benefit to the busy mom is two-fold:

1) There's less for the children to pick up at the end of the day, when they are tired and less inclined to pick up. And with less to pick up,

2) There's less difficulty getting the children to pick up or restore order to their rooms.

Children benefit.   Children benefit in three ways:

1) More time to play because there's less time spent picking up.

2) More control over possessions and a greater sense of responsibility for the care and placement of things.

3) Less time required for finding favorite toys or garments.

Easier to clean.   Finally, a tidy room is easier to dust, vacuum, and otherwise clean. Clustered items can be moved together in their storage bins, or they may not need to be moved at all. Less time spent cleaning is appreciated by both children and busy mom.

7 ● Meal Times

Just as you develop a no-fuss wardrobe for yourself and your children, strive to develop a no-fuss approach to meal times. This can happen if you make several small decisions:

Eat meals together whenever possible.

Have a set dinner time that you all can count on. Even with today's busy family schedules—and perhaps *because* of today's busy family schedules—it's more important than ever for families to spend time together. Talk about this with your children. Reach the conclusion that it's not only possible, but desirable to be together as a family on a daily basis. Make dinner time something you all come to count on as a time for sharing, laughing, and learning.

Sit down together. Turn off the television set or radio. Use this time for conversation. Dinner time can be invaluable over the course of years for developing a sense of family identity, a time to learn manners and conversational skills, and a time to share interesting and important information.

Make school lunches a shared effort.

Teach your children to clean out their lunch boxes as soon as they get home from school. Make it a game: How many seconds (use a stopwatch) does it take? Your children will have fewer reasons to offer excuses when it takes only thirty seconds to get the job done. The thermos and any other permanent containers should be rinsed and lunch boxes emptied and wiped with a damp cloth. You can wash these items more thoroughly when you do the evening dishes.

The night before, load the lunch containers that you are able to load in advance and store them in your refrigerator. Get items ready for making sandwiches—for example, set out the jar of peanut butter, a knife, and a sandwich baggie.

Teach your children to help you make school lunches. Get their input on what they like and don't like. Give them choices within the parameters of good nutrition. Use these minutes every morning to discuss the upcoming day's schedule.

Take-home food. One night a week, let your children help you decide where to go to get take-home food. Pizza, burgers, Chinese, delis—expand their horizons. Make this your no-cook night. Teach your children how to look for coupons and special offers so you can save as much money as possible. Talk about the nutritional value of various fast-food meals. Encourage your children to try new foods or menu items. All in all, use this as a time to give yourself a break from the kitchen and give your children a treat.

Dinner-time chores. Give everyone a dinnertime chore. It might be setting or clearing the table, loading or unloading the dishwasher, helping to make the salad or mashing the potatoes. Working together in the kitchen provides an opportunity for conversation and for laughter.

Your children will learn useful skills for the future and become a great help to you in the kitchen.

Assign cooking days to your teenagers.

Let each teen be responsible for cooking the evening meal one day a month. Choose the day together to accommodate both parent and teen schedules. Let your teen plan the menu, make the shopping list, and do all the cooking. As a parent, take on your teen's dinner time chore for that meal.

You'll feel less like a "chief cook and bottle washer" if you make the preparation time for meals as much a family activity as the eating time.

8 🕐 What to Wear

Decide what you and your children will wear the next day before you go to bed the night before.

Put out all the clothes your children will wear the coming day, including matching socks and shoes, hair ribbons or other accessories, and underwear.

In doing this, be sure to:

- Solicit your children's input.

- Stick with the decision the following morning.

- Use this opportunity the night before to make certain that all garments are in good repair and are clean. This goes for accessories, too.

- Think through any special events or clothing needs. Is it "jeans day" at school? Scout-uniform day?

- Pack clothing for after-school activities in a backpack or duffel bag.

This practice teaches children how to plan ahead and how to dress. You'll have opportunities to teach your children how to coordinate accessories in a more casual, less frantic mode. You'll also have more time to teach them how to mend garments, reinforce buttons, put in a hem, or clean stains. If a child's shoes need polishing, you do one and let the child do the other. If a garment needs pressing, use this opportunity to teach your child how to iron.

Wardrobe planning. By staying in touch with your children's wardrobe on a daily basis, you'll be more familiar with their wardrobe needs. You'll also be able to spot quickly whether they are maintaining good laundry room habits (see chapter 13).

Your own clothes, too. What's good for your children's morning routine is also good for yours. You'll find your own dressing goes more quickly and smoothly if you set out all your own garments the night before. Let your children help *you!* They'll find it fun to help you decide what *you* should wear and how you should accessorize.

9 ⏺ A Simple Personal Style

A first cousin to no-fuss clothing is a simplified personal style from head to toe.

A simple hairstyle. Get a good haircut that allows you maximum versatility of style and minimal upkeep. If possible, find a wash-and-wear style—one that looks good three minutes after you step out of the shower.

Help your children find a style they like and can comb and maintain with minimal, if any, help from you.

Clear nail polish. Save yourself hours a year by using clear nail polish. Carry a nail file with you, and use it when you find yourself with two or three minutes to "wait."

Limited accessories. Keep your jewelry and other accessories to a minimum. There will be less to coordinate, less to lose, less to snag, less to break, and less for toddlers and infants to pull!

Flat shoes. High heels are stylish, but they can make you feel more tired, cause harm to your feet, slow you down, and if they break, cause you all kinds of frustration and inconvenience. Try flats. At least wear them to and from events for which you feel you must wear higher heels. Flats are easier to walk in and easier to drive in (and they scuff far less).

Buy shoes that are comfortable from the first time you put them on. Don't tell yourself, I'll break them in. They'll likely break you first!

Simple makeup.   Most moms have only a few minutes a day for makeup. Keep your routine simple. Carry spare sets of travel-sized makeup containers with you in your car for quick touch-ups.

Make the most of your before-bedtime minutes.   Polish your nails, shave your legs, deep-clean your skin, and do other personal-hygiene chores in the evening, rather than the early morning. You'll feel less frantic (and have fewer razor nicks.)

10 ⏺ Good Nutrition

Good nutritional habits help you reduce everyday stress and free up your time.

Eating regular meals and healthful foods, with a minimal amount of sugar and empty calories, results in a more even blood sugar level and a steadier flow of energy for both children and adults. Which means you and your children enjoy fewer moments of feeling hungry, cranky, and utterly exhausted.

The pattern is cyclical. If you avoid ravenous moments and times of sinking fatigue, you'll be less likely to resort to fast-food fixes for energy.

Good nutritional habits can help in establishing a home that is more peaceful, with fewer arguments, less whining, and a greater sense of well-being on the part of each person.

Less sickness. Good nutritional habits, along with adequate sleep and exercise, result in less sickness and fewer chronic ailments. The immune system remains built up, the body has the elements it needs for renewal, strength is maintained, and the family as a whole experiences fewer visits to the doctor, fewer sick days, and fewer interruptions to the family's plans.

Twelve simple tips for improving your family's nutritional level.

1) Eat at regular intervals.   Set times for breakfast, lunch, and dinner. Plan for two snack times a day—one in the afternoon and one before bedtime.

2) Keep fruit on hand.   Point your children to fruit rather than to cookies or chips. Pieces of fruit last longer than fruit juices and yield more nutritional value per dollar.

3) Don't buy items high in sugar or fat.   If you keep these items out of the house, they won't be consumed!

4) Carry nutritious crackers with you in your car for a quick means of taking the edge off hunger.   A fast afterschool snack is peanut butter on whole-wheat crackers with a glass of milk.

5) Herbs and vitamins.   Explore the world of herbs and vitamins. Many products are available to help supply you and your children with the basic elements necessary for health.

6) Talk about nutrition with your children.   Let them help you read labels as you shop. Discuss the benefits of different types of foods.

7) Explore the world of spices.   Let your children experiment with you. A banana sprinkled with cinnamon? How about nutmeg on broccoli? Spices are one of the best ways to introduce your children to the world of vegetables, including salads.

8) Drink lots of water.   Keep drinking glasses at child-reach level, and make sure your children can get a drink anytime they want one. Encourage them to drink lots of water. If you're concerned about the quality of water in your area, get a water purification system.

9) Conduct periodic taste tests.   Try new foods. Adopt an attitude of exploration and experimentation.

10) Buy a bread-making machine.   The investment will come back to you over time. Your children will be fascinated at the process and love the bread.

11) Let your children help make salads.   Tearing up lettuce is something even a four-year-old can do! A child who helps make a salad is a child more likely to eat a salad.

12) Pop corn.   For a quick snack, pop a bag of popcorn in the microwave. Any child can master the skill. Unbuttered, unsalted popcorn is nutritious and filling. It's got a great shelf life, too.

One final tip: avoid chewing gum. It can promote tooth decay and create all kinds of messes.

11 🌒 Mommy Kits

There are some things a mom should have tucked away in her purse. At least, there are some things children *think* their moms should have and some things busy moms are *wise* to have on hand.

Satchels, not purses. Mothers carry bags, not dainty little purses. Find a tote or satchel that you can sling over your shoulder, and get used to carrying the weight. You may want to have a tiny clutch you can withdraw for a quick dash into a convenience store.

This does *not* mean you need to be the pack animal for the entire family. Other family members can carry backpacks and child-sized purses. It *does* mean you probably will find that life goes more smoothly if you have ready access at all times to the following items:

- *Facial tissues.* A small dispenser's worth or pop-up wipes.

- *Scissors.* Big enough to clip a loose thread, a hangnail, or a coupon.

- *Sewing kit.* A tiny one from a hotel will probably do. Add a couple of safety pins (in different sizes) and a few straight pins if they aren't already a part of the kit.

- *Band-Aids.* A few in various sizes. Tuck them in an old prescription-style pill bottle (after removing the label).

- *Emergency phone call money and numbers.* Keep money for two or three phone calls and your important emergency numbers in a small coin purse apart from your regular wallet. (Keep change for parking meters and road tolls separate from phone-call change.)

- *Medication.* Carry an extra round of required medication with you in case you don't get home on time. Keep a few aspirin-free pain pills handy.

- *Crayons and paper.* A small pad of paper and a sandwich-size ziplock baggie filled with crayons can provide instant entertainment for children during times of unexpected waiting.

- *Dental floss.* It comes in handy as "string" or "thread" in an emergency and helps maintain hygiene if you and your children find yourselves enduring a non-stop day.

- *A brush and comb* (suitable for your children's hair).

- *Extra rubber bands, paper clips, hair clips, and shoelaces.* Put them in a baggie or small zippered container.

As mentioned previously, carry your calendar with you and a couple of pens, too.

If you have a teenage daughter, keep a spare means of feminine hygiene with you in a discreet container.

12 ● Establish Designated Places

Designate places for items that families tend to spend a great deal of time looking for, usually when they are in the greatest hurry.

Have a place where you always put

- *Your keys.* Hang a key rack near the door or use a small dish to hold your car and house keys. Eliminate unnecessary keys from your ring. Always label seldom-used keys with tags for quick reference.

- *Mail.* Have a place where the day's mail is deposited within the house, no matter who goes to the mailbox to get it.

- *Messages.* Have a place (perhaps a bulletin board) where you can leave messages for other family members.

- *Items brought home from school.* This designated place might be the same one where you leave family messages. Teach your children to bring school announcements to your attention immediately.

- *Lunch money.* Have a place where your children know they can pick up their lunch money.

- *Lunch boxes.* Have a place where lunch boxes are left for refilling.

In addition to creating these designated spaces, teach your children to:

- Put trash in trash cans or wastepaper baskets.
- Hang up clothes.
- Rinse off dishes after their use.
- Put rinsed-but-not-washed dirty dishes in a sink of soapy water.

Designated spaces spare you frustration, and you and your family will have a sense of greater order in your home.

13 ● Dirty-Clothes Hampers

It's important to designate a place in your home for dirty-clothes hampers or baskets. Make it a rule that all family members use them (even the little ones).

Invest in several laundry baskets. They may be the kind you can stack to save space or the tall and deep trash-can style.

Label one basket or hamper for whites, one for colored garments, and one for towels.

Train your children to sort their own garments and towels into these baskets on a daily basis. Consider adopting this general principle:

> *As soon as a garment comes off,*
> *it goes either*
> *1) into the closet or drawer, or*
> *2) into the dirty-clothes hampers.*

Ask your children to help you fold towels and to put clean clothes away. Make "doing the laundry" an activity you do together, subtly teaching all aspects of the chore along the way.

As soon as your child reaches the age of eight, start cycling laundry onto his or her chore list. A child at that age can learn to load a washing machine, measure the soap, set the dials, and make the transfer to a dryer.

Children will develop discipline and a sense of order by helping you with the laundry, and you'll save hours of picking up scattered socks and undies and spend less time in the laundry room!

14 ● Home-Free Nights

Do you remember the cry, "Ollie, Ollie, home free!" that was part of playing hide 'n' seek? The idea is valuable for busy moms!

Have at least one kick-back, nothing-scheduled, no-pressure evening set aside each week. Be "home free"—no running to the store or laundromat; no going out to a meeting; no soccer practice or play rehearsal.

Even better, schedule yourself a home-free day occasionally—yes, even a Saturday or Sunday. Push the chores and errands to another time. Ignore the call of the car keys. Refuse to be enticed out of the house.

Off with the makeup.

On with the lounge clothes.

Unplug the phone (if you dare, and if you don't have teenagers) or at least let the answering machine do the answering for you.

Turn off the tube.

And unwind.

Home-free activities for the entire family.

"But, what will we DO?" you may ask. The answer is simple: play together as a family.

- Pull out the old board games or cards.

- Get on the floor and play with your children's toys, with your children!

- Read books together. If your children are small, read to them. If they're older have them read to you. If they're teens, photocopy a play in anticipation of such a night—yes, even Shakespeare—and read it together, each person taking a part or parts.

- Get out the clay or paints or crayons and create something.

- Play catch in the backyard. Or volleyball. Or hopscotch. Or jump rope.

Use your playtime as an opportunity to talk, and above all, to laugh together. Tell jokes. Make up funny plot lines.

And as the night draws to a close, have a rip-roaring pillow fight. You'll all sleep better.

15 🕐 Streamlined Grocery Shopping

Conduct your own family survey. How many hours a week do you spend going to, shopping in, and coming home from grocery and discount family stores (such as Wal-Mart, Kmart, Target)? Don't be shocked if you discover that you are making a daily run or are spending more than six hours a week buying food and sundries.

You can streamline this chore, saving yourself hours, dollars, and frustration. Here are four simple and practical things to try:

1) Make lists. Keep a running grocery and sundry list. Plan a week's menus in advance. Check to make sure you have, or have on the list, all the things you'll need for at least five dinners, seven breakfasts, and five school lunches. (You'll probably eat one meal out or purchase take-out food, and at least one dinner a week is likely to be a time for leftovers). It will only take you five to ten minutes to sketch a meal plan for the coming week and to list the ingredients you need.

Have a family policy, such as:

> *If you see that we're running out*
> *of something, put it on the list!*

This goes for everything from peanut butter to toothpaste. Any family member should have the prerogative to put something on the grocery list! (You can always opt not to buy the item.)

2) Shop only once a week.   Discipline yourself to make only one grocery run a week. If you need milk or other perishables in between times, use convenience stores on your way to or from work.

3) Shop during off hours.   Evening hours and Saturday mornings are times when the grocery stores tend to be less crowded.

One family I know takes a cooler with them and uses it to store perishables. That way, they can hit the grocery store first—ahead of the crowds—on their Saturday morning errand run and still make it home with unmelted ice cream.

Grocery shopping can actually be a fun family outing. Make it a challenge. Divide the list and send the children on missions to collect specific items. Ask each child to make choices between two similar products, comparing labels and unit prices. Give yourself a time goal. Discuss new and interesting products that you spot along the aisles. Talk to the grocers, especially in the vegetable and meat areas of a market. Have your children ask the butcher or green grocer, What can we make with this? How should we cook this? What goes good with this? Such information keeps your children's minds engaged in something other than the freebies in the cereal boxes.

4) Consider home delivery.   A number of prepackaged-meal delivery services are available in most major cities (beyond Chinese food and pizza). Some of these companies offer everything from casseroles to desserts, with a real home-cooked taste to the foods. A few dairies will still deliver milk products to your door. And some grocery stores take orders over the phone and deliver; all for a fee of course. Still, if time is more important to you than money, home delivery is worth considering.

16. Assign Chores

Every person in a family should have specific chores for which they are responsible.

Chores are tasks that are done on a periodic basis for the benefit of the *entire* family. (Making one's bed and emptying one's wastepaper basket are "chores" in that they help maintain a greater sense of household order and cleanliness. By comparison, brushing one's own teeth is *not* a chore.)

Every child age five and older can do one or two chores a day. Little ones might bring in the newspaper or mail. Teens can run a vacuum and dust once a week, or start a load of laundry every morning.

- *Post chore lists.* Assign specific tasks to specific children. Post a new list every week. Most children have difficulty envisioning a task-period longer than a week.

- *Set deadlines or times.* If the trash goes out Monday and Thursday, mark that on the chore list. If you want the child's bed made before breakfast, say so.

- *Set standards for excellence.* Teach your children the difference between a neatly made bed and a sloppily made bed. Show them *how* to rake the leaves.

A Sample Chore List

	Katie (age 8)	Annie (age 6)	Craig (age 10)
MONDAY	Make bed before school Feed cat	Make bed before school Water cat	Make bed before school Feed fish
TUESDAY	Make bed before school Feed cat	Make bed before school Water cat	Make bed before school Feed fish
WEDNESDAY	Put sheets in wash Feed cat	Make bed before school Water cat	Make bed before school Feed fish
THURSDAY	Make bed before school Feed cat	Put sheets in wash Water cat	Make bed before school Feed fish
FRIDAY	Make bed before school Feed cat	Make bed before school Water cat	Put sheets in wash Feed fish
SATURDAY	Make bed Feed cat	Make bed Water cat	Make bed Feed fish

Expect chores to be completed with a sense of responsibility and care.

- *Rotate some chores.* Give everybody a chance to do the least favorite or the easiest chore.

- *Keep track of work completed.* Check marks or stars next to a list give children a sense of accomplishment and completion. Parents, not children, should mark off work completed.

- *Reward good work.* Establish rewards. They may be related to quality or to the fact that the chores are done without a parent's asking. Don't reward sloppy or careless work, and don't reward the completion of chores if you must ask a child to do the chore more than once.

- *List your own chores as a parent.* If your children are feeling "put upon" by the work you are requiring of them, list the chores that you do as a parent. Your children will probably be delighted at having so little to do by comparison!

- *Praise your children for doing chores.* Say thank you to your children. Rewards are related to tasks. Praise is for the *child.* Tell them frequently how much you appreciate their help.

Chores help build discipline and responsibility in children, and they provide a means for lessening a busy mom's work load.

17 ● Cluster Appointments

When making dental, pediatric, or other periodic appointments for your children, group them together. Better to sit with two children for forty-five minutes in the doctor's office than to make two trips, each for a half hour!

When you go shoe shopping, go with everyone and buy for everyone. You might have two or three clerks waiting on you, but the process will be far more fun and more streamlined if everyone is trying on shoes.

When the time comes for haircuts, book appointments back to back.

As parent-teacher conference times approach, ask your children's teachers to work with you so you only need to make one trip to the school. You might want to talk with each teacher at the beginning of the year, and give each teacher a note or card with the time on it when you would *like* to come for a conference. (That way, you're pretty much in charge of your own scheduling and you're likely to have your request granted because you have asked so far in advance.)

Ask for your children's piano or tutoring lessons to be scheduled back to back.

Look for soccer teams that practice at the same fields, or Little League teams that use the same park facilities on the same days.

Your goal as a busy mom is to make fewer trips and spend less time in waiting rooms!

18 🕐 Take-Along Bags

Keep a "take-along" bag in your car for each child, or if you use public transportation, have a backpack for each child.

Consider this an activity bag, with items your children can use to entertain themselves quietly while they're in waiting rooms, in transit, or at other times when they are bored.

Each bag should be small and portable, with carrying handles, and should include such items as:

- Colored pencils and a small pencil sharpener. (Since the bags are likely to be in the car at all times, avoid items that may melt, such as crayons.)

- A pad of plain paper.

- A coloring book.

- A couple of small games, such as a peg-style chess board, a magnetic checkers set, or a deck of cards.

- A book of puzzles or travel-game activities.

Choose items that can be played quietly, don't require conversation, and have self-storage containers. Don't choose items that are battery operated or have lots of pieces.

Games of Imagination

A to Z and I Spy are wonderful ways to occupy a child's imagination while standing in line, sitting in a waiting room, or traveling by car.

A to Z

A to Z is played this way: One person chooses the category and gives the first line (see below). Each person must then repeat the line and supply a word in alphabetical order. For example, a person might say, "I'm so hungry I could eat an avocado," and the next two people might say, "I'm so hungry I could eat a banana" and "I'm so hungry I could eat a carrot."

A variation on the game is to require each person to repeat all of the items that have preceded her or his item. ("I'm so hungry I could eat an avocado, a banana, a carrot, and a/an—.")

I Spy

I Spy is played this way: One person says, "I spy something—" and names a category and then cites an item that fits the category. For example, the person might say, "I spy something red. I spy a red ball." Each person must then find something that color to spy—such as "I spy a red jacket" or "I spy red lipstick."

A variation on the game is to make it a guessing game. A person says, "I spy something—" and gives one clue about an item everyone can see. The person continues to give clues until someone guesses what the object is. In taking turns, the person whose item requires the most clues from the other player wins.

A "bag of imagination."   There will be times when even an activity bag becomes boring. Teach your children to use those times to make up stories and to use their imaginations to wile away the time. An empty brown paper sack can become a "bag of imagination." Children can take turns imagining what could be in the bag—from a herd of elephants to a sixteen-scoop ice-cream cone.

As a busy mom, you don't have time to, energy to, aren't likely to want to, or may not be available to play referee, tour guide, entertainer, or problem-solver for most of the hours in your children's lives. Teach them to provide their own amusement—quietly, safely, and imaginatively.

A bag of dry clothes.   Consider keeping a small zippered tote bag in the back of your car or van, with a complete set of dry clothes for each child. If your child has a major spill, falls into a puddle, rips a garment, or gets sick, you'll be prepared.

19 🕐 Personalized Bedtimes

Bedtime can be one of the coziest, most meaningful times of the day for a child and for a mom-child relationship.

Make bedtime something special.

First and foremost, make a promise to yourself that you'll be there for your children's bedtime. If you're away from home, be sure to call.

Spend a few minutes alone with *each* child. Let your child count on this as a time when he or she has your undivided, unhurried attention.

You may want to read a story together, say a prayer together, or talk over the day a little. (Again, if you're away from home, you can still do all these things over the phone.)

Hug your child; sit close as you share this time together.

Quality communication. Many working moms feel guilty about not spending enough "quality time" with their children. Rather than think in terms of quality time, think in terms of "quantity time" and "quality communication."

Bedtime conversation should be a time for quality communication with these hallmarks:

- *Listen to your child.* If he or she mentions a problem during a bedtime prayer, don't gloss over it. Take time to explore the situation and your child's feelings about it.

- *No issue or topic should be off limits.*

- *Explore feelings and opinions, reasons and ideas.* Ask your child leading open-ended questions.

- *Apologize if you feel you have hurt your child in some way.* (At the same time, don't back down on discipline or unload feelings or reasons that may be too great an emotional burden for your child to carry.)

Bring the day to a close with peace. Assure your children of your nearby presence through the night hours.

Bedtime is the one time of day when busy moms should choose not to be busy, and working moms should avoid all thoughts of work. Fifteen minutes with your children at this time of day, every day, is valuable beyond measure.

20⏱ Arm Your Children with Information

Make sure your children know what they need to know.

They should know their full names and parents' full names.

They should have key phone numbers memorized. (Each child's name and phone number should be put on a name tag attached to his or her backpack or school bag.)

They should know their pediatrician's name.

They should know the name of where you and your husband work (and if the organization is a large one, in which department or division).

What to do in an emergency. Talk to your children in advance about what they should do in these crisis situations:

- *If your child gets separated from you while you are shopping together or are traveling together.* (The best solution is for your child to stop and stand still, or sit down, and count to at least one hundred.)

- *If you don't show up on time.* (Whom should your children call? With whom may they leave the scene? Where should they wait?)

- *If they are home without adult supervision.* Give your children coping skills—how to lock doors, what to do if they sense danger, how to close curtains.

Vital Information

Your child should know the following information by the time he or she is three years old and should be able to give it to an adult in authority in a clear, loud, easily-understood voice:

☐ Full name (first and last names)
☐ Home address (house number, street, and city)
☐ Home telephone number
☐ Mother's name (first and last names)
☐ Father's name (first and last names)
☐ Doctor's name (last name)
☐ Mother's employer (company name)
☐ Father's employer (company name)

Your child should be able to identify these adult authority figures:

- A police officer   • A fire fighter
- A store clerk   • A doctor
- A school-crossing   • A security guard
  guard

Your child should be able to identify

- A stop sign   • A danger sign (skull
- A do-not-enter   and crossbones)
  sign

- *If they get home before you do.* Make sure your children know how to get in the house if they arrive home to find all the doors and windows locked. Or, make certain they know where to go and wait for you to arrive.

- *If they are approached by a stranger or sense danger.* Make sure they know that it's OK to run, OK to scream, OK to say no.

- *If they see a gun, are in a fire, hurt themselves, and so forth.* Take on emergency situations one by one and talk your way through them.

Make sure your children know how to dial 911 or where to find emergency phone numbers in case the police or an ambulance is needed.

Rehearse this information.   Don't assume that because you told your children something one time, they will remember it forever. Information such as this must be rehearsed repeatedly. A good time to go over safety information—as well as general information—is while traveling by car together. Make it a "what should you do if?" game. Or, ask questions in a gamelike way:
"Who loves you more than anybody?"
"You do!"
"Who am I?"
"Mommy"
But what is Mommy's name?"
"Kate Redd."
"And how do you reach Mommy so she can tell you that she loves you?"
"I call her on the phone."

"What number do you call?"
And so forth.

Arm your children with information in a preventive, reassuring way. Such information can keep them from panic or emotional trauma. More important, it can save their lives, literally.

21 ● Home Safety

A busy mom, especially a mom who is away from home a great deal of the time, will feel less stress if she knows she has made her home as safe as possible for her children.

An annual safety audit. Once a year, make a thorough audit of your home, with safety in mind. Get on your hands and knees and see the world from your children's point of view. Which cupboards and drawers can they get into? In those cupboards and drawers, what poses a danger to them? What can you do to secure these spaces or to remove the danger? What about electrical cords, slippery carpets, unsecured electrical outlets, house plants, and draping table covers?

Change the batteries in the smoke detector. Check the date on the fire extinguisher. Check the location and security of all chemical solutions in the bathroom, kitchen, and garage.

Engage your children in the process. You can turn the safety audit into a detective game. Give your children a goal: identify the ten most dangerous things in your house.

Secure windows and doors. Make certain that you have burglar-proof devices on your windows and sliding glass doors, and that you have appropriate dead-bolt locks on all outside doors (properly installed).

Mark the windows of children's bedrooms. A simple red circle on outside windows tells emergency crews which rooms are occupied by children.

Fire drills. Go over emergency procedures with your children should the smoke detector sound its alarm. Practice evacuation procedures.

Medicine cabinets. Keep prescription medications and any dangerous chemicals stored in a locked medicine cabinet.

Shop and garden tools and electrical appliances. Make sure these items are stored out of reach of little hands.

As a busy mom, you know you can't be everywhere your children are. Do your best to seal off danger and instruct your children about dangers and emergency procedures.

22 ● Cook Double Portions

Would you like to double your cooking output with only ten percent more effort? You can!

The trick is in doubling a recipe and freezing the portion you don't need immediately. If you have large cooking pots, you may be able to triple a recipe and prepare three times the food for less than twenty percent more effort.

This is especially good for foods such as:

- Casseroles, including lasagne and enchiladas.

- Soups, stews, and chili.

- Homemade spaghetti sauce and sloppy-joe concoctions.

If you're preparing mashed potatoes, it only takes a couple of minutes to boil an extra potato or two. Use the extras the next day to make a potato salad, or mash the entire lot and save the leftovers for shepherd's pie later in the week.

If you're baking, double the recipe for cookies or bread dough. Freeze the extra baked goods for later use.

Virtually any recipe that can be frozen will work for this plan. Serve a regular meal portion from your large pot, cool the remainder, ladle it into freezer-worthy, meal-sized containers, label the containers (for quick identification later), put them in the freezer, and consider that dinner has already been fixed for that unforeseen night when you feel too tired to breathe, much less cook.

Granted, there are four things you need to make this system work with maximum efficiency:

1) A freezer. You may want to invest in a 12- or 14-cubic-foot freezer. You'll get your investment back many times over.

2) Freezer-worthy containers in a variety of sizes. Choose square shapes. They store more compactly in a freezer.

3) A microwave oven. The system also works with conventional ovens; just pull your main course out of the freezer in the morning and let it defrost all day in the refrigerator.

4) A plan-ahead approach to meal preparation. The benefits are tremendous!

Once you're in the habit of cooking double portions, you'll find you can put at least *half* of your evening meals on the table almost instantly.

Slow cooking. Sometimes the fastest way to prepare a meal is to cook it slowly! Dig out the Crockpot and get acquainted with some of the new recipe books that are available.

Consider cooking a turkey on low heat overnight. You'll have enough turkey for several meals and probably some to freeze.

Saturday cooking sprees. Have you ever noticed how many of your favorite recipes use the same ingredients, with only slight variations? Buy in bulk (which usually means a cost savings) or in large sizes, and devote one Saturday a month to a cooking spree. The entire family can pitch in. Over the course of several hours, you can easily make up to twenty or thirty meal-sized portions—just by keeping the oven hot and your largest kettles simmering.

23 • Turn Down the Volume

Noise causes stress. Noise requires attention, and attention takes effort, and effort drains energy. In our overlystimulating world, most of us could benefit from less stimuli, not more.

Therefore, to reduce stress and to have more energy—for yourself and your entire family—reduce the noise level!

Keep the radio off. If you must have music, sing. Singing reduces stress and releases tension.

At home, keep the stereo turned down low or keep it off. Play music that is soothing or appealing to every member of your family.

Turn off the television set. After your family has made it through the detoxification stage (usually about a week) you'll be amazed at the peace that settles over your home. Individual creativity is likely to be reborn. After a month of no television or highly limited television viewing, you may be amazed that you ever had the time to watch so much TV. (If you need suggestions about alternative activities, consider getting a copy of *52 Things for Your Kids to Do Instead of Watching TV.*)

If you must watch the news, try limiting yourself to half

an hour of news a day. There's little likelihood that you need to watch or listen to more news than that. Most of the information on news broadcasts is not information the average person can act upon or apply to his or her everyday life. You may find that you feel personally calmer as the result of watching less news. A steady stream of visual images and descriptions of violence, problems, and natural disasters can create an inner tension that has no outlet for release.

Many parents find that a no-TV policy (or a highly regulated viewing policy) results in their children playing more cooperatively and with less hyperactivity. The children benefit by not having the steady diet of fast-paced violent behaviors so common to much of children's programming. They're likely to use their imaginations more and to have a greater opportunity for developing interpersonal skills. As a parent, you'll also find that you're subjected to a lot less "buy me" pressure from your children.

Speak in a lower tone of voice.   Many family members are so accustomed to yelling over the noise of television sets, radios, or stereos that they don't even realize they are talking louder than necessary. Try lowering the volume at the dinner table. Discuss this noise-reduction experiment with your children. It may take a little practice, but you're likely to find that dinner with a lower volume level is more enjoyable and more conducive to good digestion.

Don't shout at your children to get their attention. Motion for them to come close enough for you to speak to them in a normal tone of voice. You'll probably find that they respond better to your instructions or comments.

They're also likely to be close enough for the occasional spontaneous hug!

Turn down the volume on your life, and you're likely to hear its messages more clearly.

24 ⏱ Child-High Essentials

A busy mom can save herself lots of interruptions if she adjusts certain essentials in her home to the height of her children!

Keep a footstool in the kitchen and bathroom so your children can reach the sinks.

Keep bathroom supplies such as toothbrushes and toothpaste, extra rolls of toilet tissue, and hand soap within your children's reach.

Keep drinking glasses within easy reach, and make drinking water readily available. You may need to adapt a water dispenser so your children can always get a drink when they want it—without your assistance.

Adjust the shelves, racks, and rods in your children's closets so they can reach their clothes. Keep underwear, socks, and other clothing items in lower drawers or bins.

Install an extra towel rack in the bathroom at child height. (You may also want to have a towel rack or a paper towel dispenser at child height in the kitchen.)

Put Peg-Boards or hang-up rods at your children's level in the porch, mud room, or entry way so they can hang up their own coats, rain gear, or backpacks.

Booster seats.   Children who are too big for infant car seats or high chairs, yet too small to see out the car window or over the edge of the dining table, are at a disadvantage. Invest in appropriate booster seats so your children can fully participate in your family and see what *you* see.

25 ⏱ Have a Backup Child-Care Plan

As you interview and hire baby sitters, develop a relationship with two or three sitters. Alternate among them. You'll be in a better position when a crisis strikes or you need a sitter on short notice.

As you do the necessary research for choosing child-care assistance—whether a part-time child-care service, a full-time child-care center or preschool, or a full-time nanny or baby sitter—be sure to ask these questions:

1) What about sick days? Does the day-care center provide a means for caring for sick children? Is there a sick-child facility or service in your area, perhaps one sponsored by a local hospital or clinic?

2) What about late pick-ups? If you can't arrive at the normal pick-up time, what options are available to your children? What provisions do you need to make to ensure that they have a place to go?

You're going to need these Plan B backup procedures. Anticipate them in advance. Your children *will* get sick. You *will* be late to pick up your children from preschool, school, or a child-care center on occasion. Find a child-care provider who will work with you to develop the most foolproof Plan B possible.

Consider some of these options:

- *After-school activity centers or child-care services.* Sometimes these centers are located adjacent to elementary school campuses or are housed within a school building.

- *Exchanging late pick-ups with a neighbor or friend.*

- *Carpooling with others in your neighborhood.*

- *Calling a nearby Christian college for a list of qualified students for part-time employment.* Some colleges have a published baby-sitter list. Consider hiring a reliable college student to pick up your children from school and spend a couple of after-school hours with them every day. Education majors frequently have a special talent for helping children get a jump on the evening's homework or for promoting creative play.

- *Asking your pastor, priest, or rabbi for names of persons in your church community who are interested in periodic or part-time child-care work.* See if there are persons in your faith community who are willing to form a baby-sitting pool for emergency or sick-child situations.

26 🕐 A Day at a Time

Children live in the moment.

Therefore, for their sake and for the benefit of your entire family, live one day at a time.

In the morning. Take a few minutes to talk about the day's activities with your children. Remind them of any changes in the normal routine, such as a special event planned for the late afternoon or evening. If they need to be home at a certain time, give them specific instructions. Tell your children in detail what you expect them to do and ask them to repeat your instructions to you. Don't assume that your children will remember a change of schedule you discussed yesterday or last week.

Go over each child's schedule. Make notes. Your child will be delighted to see you are taking his or her upcoming day so seriously. You'll feel more in touch with your child by recording his or her agenda where you can refer to it during the day. If your child has a math test at ten o'clock, your note about it can remind you to pray for him during that hour and ask him how the test went when you talk to him after school.

At mid-day. Contact your children sometime during the day; perhaps a phone call after school. Or establish a procedure whereby your children call you within a half hour of arriving home. Spend a few minutes going over the highlights of the day. You'll have a lot more peace knowing that your children are home safely.

Even if your children are in a day-care center on a full-time basis, stop by occasionally to share lunch with them or to watch them play at recess. If they are in high school, a periodic lunch off campus with Mom can be a real treat.

In the evening. As you fix dinner with your children or share the evening meal, talk over the day's events. Listen to what happened in the life of each person. Share what you experienced. You'll likely find that as you keep the communication lines open on a daily, practical, life-sharing basis, your children will feel more comfortable in coming to you during times of crisis.

27 ● A Place for Everybody

You can save lots of time over the course of a decade or so of childrearing, if you designate "places."

Have a set place at the dinner table for each person. When you eat out, gravitate toward those same positions around a table.

Have a set place in the car or van for each person. You may want to rotate the seating positions occasionally so everyone has a turn at a window seat or a front seat.

Have a plan for who will sit where *before* you enter the church sanctuary, the movie theater, the concert, or the ball park. Give everyone a chance periodically at the aisle seat.

Whenever possible, spare yourself the role of referee and seat an adult between two children, rather than letting two children sit side by side.

A place to be alone. Every person in a family needs a place to call "my spot." Be sure to provide such a place for each child, no matter how young he or she may be. This should be a place where your child feels free to go when feeling sad, overwhelmed, cramped for space, or just to be alone for a few minutes. Make sure others respect the privacy of each person's privileged space. Although you may limit the amount of time a person spends in solitude, don't limit the access to it. Everybody needs to know they can "get by themselves" if they need to.

28 🕐 Don't Try to Do It All

This tip is for the entire family! Don't try to do everything.

Don't try to see the whole zoo in one outing. See a portion of it and save the rest for another day.

Don't try to ride every ride at the amusement park or hit all parts of the fair in one evening. Pick out a few things to do, see, or ride, and consider the outing a success.

Don't feel as if you need to walk every path or climb on every piece of play equipment at the park. Learn to enjoy just a piece of the action to the max.

If you are taking your children to an evening performance such as a concert or variety show, give yourself permission to leave at intermission time.

As you map out your vacation itinerary, don't try to hit everything listed in your travel book as something worthy of your attention. Pick out some highlights appropriate for the ages of your children and be satisfied.

By cramming too many events into too short a time, you and your children will soon hit overload. The event will take on tension it wouldn't otherwise have. You and your children will get overly tired with the resulting frayed nerves and tears. And rather than "do" the event in a way that is pleasant and fun, the event may well do *you* in.

The true value of an outing lies in what each person

learns from it and what the mutual sharing of an experience does to build a total family relationship. Events in which one is *pressured* to learn and do, see and experience, ultimately are unpleasant and deteriorate rather than enrich relationships.

When you leave a place knowing you haven't done it all, keep the family conversation focused on what you *did* experience rather than what you didn't experience.

Let your children know in advance that you aren't going to try to do everything, but that you will be picking and choosing some things to do and see. Just as you don't order everything offered on a menu each time you go to a restaurant, so you can't do everything in any one place.

By adopting this approach to family experiences, you will find your children are ultimately more satisfied with life in general. They will be learning to sample experiences, without developing a compulsion to experience everything. They'll feel rewarded, rather than cheated. And they'll have something to look forward to during future visits or during their own travels as an adult with *their* families.

29 ● Choose Child-Friendly Places

Choose, as best you can, to go to "child-friendly" places during the years when your children are small.

The gourmet restaurants and formal events will still be there when your children are grown or when you and your spouse are on a date alone.

Stick to places that cater to children and appreciate them as customers, clients, and observers.

Visit the children's museums or the hands-on art galleries that invite your children to touch items, manipulate levers and pulleys, conduct experiments, and above all, to talk about what they see.

Eat at restaurants that offer a child's menu with good variety and foods with wholesome nutritional value. (It *is* possible.) This does not mean that you need to limit yourself to fast-food restaurants. Children can learn good table manners and enjoy lovely family restaurants.

As you plan your vacation:

- Choose accommodations that have playgrounds or swimming pools so your children have a place to expend pent-up energy.

- Consider spending your vacation at a resort (or on a cruise ship) that has a special program just for children, such as play equipment, supervised play, and snack bars.

- Look for restaurants that are near parks or beaches so your children can take a walk or spend a little time in play during a break in the day's travel.

- Choose activities that are fun for your children. For example, your children may not enjoy shopping in the elegant stores of San Francisco, but they will enjoy riding the cable cars, feeding the pigeons in the central plaza, and watching the boats at Fisherman's Wharf.

Go to events aimed at children, such as children's theaters, the children's concert series presented by your local symphony, puppet shows, circus performances, stage plays, and ice-skating shows with a children's motif. You will expose your children to a great deal of culture with all the fun and none of the pain.

30 🕐 Limit the Parties

Just as you don't need to do it all as an adult or as a family, your children don't need to "attend them all" when it comes to parties.

Count the number of parties each of your children attended last year. How much did these parties cost you? You may be surprised to see just how much time, money, and effort children's parties are taking in your life.

I recently asked a young mother to do this for her children—all under the age of twelve. She recalled at least twenty birthday and back-to-school parties, not to mention the get togethers at the close of soccer and baseball seasons. Plus the birthday parties she hosted for each child.

She estimated that she spent close to $300 a year on gifts for her children to take to parties, and about $80 for each of the parties she hosted.

The costs in terms of money and time weren't limited to the gifts and parties themselves, of course. Several of the parties required costumes or new outfits for her children. Which meant more time shopping and more expense.

Was it all necessary? "No," she said. Was it really worth it? Again, she said, "No." Is she likely to be involved in more than twenty parties again this coming year? "Probably. I don't know how to get off this merry-go-round," she admitted.

If you find yourself on a party treadmill with no "off" switch try the following:

- Get together with some of the mothers of your children's friends to discuss this issue. They may be just as happy as you are to curtail the parties, in number and in scope.

- Don't promise your children a birthday party every year. A "milestone" birthday party—say at ages five, twelve, sixteen—may be more meaningful than a party each year. You can limit annual celebrations to family, with simple birthday cakes and your child's favorite meal.

- Say no to some invitations. Plan something else for you and your children to do on the party day so that they have both a fun activity and a good excuse if asked later by their playmates why they weren't in attendance.

Minimize the event.   If you can't put a stop to the round of parties, at least minimize your loss of time and money.

- Buy general gifts on sale as you see them.

- Cut back on decorations.

- Buy a large roll of butcher paper to use as all-purpose wrapping paper, or a bundle of plain colored gift bags and packets of brightly colored tissue paper.

- Keep the party outdoors if possible. There will be less mess to clean up and less potential damage to your home. Let the children play outdoor games. Have simple competitions. Keep the dress casual.

- Limit the guest list.

- Let your children make the invitations and deliver them by hand.

31 ● Limit the Guest Traffic

Just as you limit the number of parties your children host or attend, you can also limit the number of friends your children invite into your home.

Let your children invite one or two friends over for an afternoon of play—not an entire gang of children.

Limit the number of extra mouths you feed. Insist that your children ask in advance whether they can invite a friend over for lunch or dinner. Set quotas—perhaps one guest a week, rotating among your children the privilege of inviting a friend to dinner. The fewer the friends who are invited to dinner, the greater the opportunity for the entire family to get to know each child.

Control the number of children you take along with you on an outing or shopping. Do you really want to be responsible for more children at the mall?

Make sleep-over occasions more special by limiting the times a child may invite a friend to spend the night. Again, have only one outside guest over per night. If each child has a sleep-over friend on the same night, there's little likelihood of peaceful interaction among the sets of children or of a peaceful night's sleep for you as a parent.

The emphasis is on *limiting,* not eliminating. Guests are fun. Hospitality is important. Friendships are invaluable. The point is that you are a busy mom with hardly enough time to build relationships with your own children. Adding more children to the process further reduces the time you can spend with each child.

Be assured, you aren't depriving your children of social opportunities or friendships by limiting the access to your family. You are preserving the identity of your family and fostering opportunities for better communication among your own children.

Limit the foot traffic.

Limit the spaces in your home in which you allow children to play or congregate. Certain rooms or areas may be off-limits. As much as possible (within the constraints of weather and safety), insist that children play outside. It's better for them physically and socially, and it lessens the wear and tear on the house.

Insist that all children walk, not run, in the house and that they close doors behind them without slamming them. Insist that they choose to be outside or inside—not back and forth.

32 🕐 Waiting Games

Even the busiest family has moments of waiting. The wait in lines in stores and drive-through windows may be only a few minutes, but to a child, each minute can seem like twenty.

Unfortunately, most children don't wait well. They haven't yet learned the skill of disengagement or daydreaming that adults have cultivated. Their first impulse is to generate activity.

This activity will be physical or mental. Your goal is to keep the activity mental. Physical activity is likely to be rough-housing—punching, hitting, jabbing either a person or an object.

Develop a repertoire of songs, word games, and quizzes to employ during waiting moments:

- *Memory work.* What are your children currently memorizing? It may be the alphabet, numbers from one to one hundred, multiplication tables, Scriptures or a poem. Use waiting minutes for rehearsal.

- *Q & A.* Ask your children questions to rehearse safety instructions or family rules.

    Questions and answers may also relate to specific subjects or categories that your children are currently studying in school such as states and their capitals.

- *Math problems.* Give your children math equations to complete. Rather than have a free-for-all competition for answer privileges, ask each child a question in turn.

- *Songs.* Sing together. Turn waiting time into rehearsal time!

- *"I Spy."* You can relate the game to items outside the car or around you. You can set up categories related to people you know as a family, Bible characters, rooms in your house, places at school, areas of your church.

- *The Alphabet Game.* Pick a genre and take turns coming up with the name of something that begins with each succeeding letter of the alphabet. For example, choose foods and put together a string of artichokes, bananas, cherries, dip, enchiladas, and so forth.

- *Jokes and riddles.* Share jokes, riddles, and funny stories with one another. Embarrassing-moment stories can also bring a laugh.

Fill up the waiting moments of your lives with meaningful words and laughter. Seize opportunities to talk together where you find them. Don't overlook these golden waiting moments.

33 ⏰ Stay on a Family Schedule

As much as possible, adopt a family schedule and stick to it. Life will be more orderly for all of you. Rather than feeling confined by a schedule, you and your children will more likely feel that there's a regularity and a rhythm to your relationship and your function as a family unit.

Early to rise. Establish a getting-up time for your children. Allow sufficient time for them to dress and get ready personally, to make their beds, to gather their school supplies, to have a good breakfast, and to have a little devotional time before leaving for school or beginning their day of play. Don't race through the morning. This actually can be a great time for children to practice, too—perhaps fifteen minutes at the piano or a typewriter. (One child might practice while another showers and makes the bed; then they can trade off.)

How can you train a child to arise early enough for all this to take place and feel thoroughly rested and ready to go? By setting a suitable bedtime for each child!

Early to bed. Establish a going-to-bed time for each person. Adjust it periodically for each child as he or she matures. Keep in mind that children need nine to ten hours of sleep a night to have the maximum amount of energy during the day.

Don't let television programming dictate your children's going-to-bed time. Instead, work backward from the getting-up time you establish as a family. Early to bed will make early to rise a cinch.

Even if your children aren't dog-tired or even very sleepy at the designated bedtime, insist that they get ready for bed and curl up under the covers. Spend a few minutes with each child for bedtime prayers, in quiet conversation, for goodnight hugs and kisses. You might let your children read by themselves for a few minutes before lights out. Let them know they can always use those alone times before sleep comes to daydream or make up stories.

Meals.   Keep meals at fairly regular intervals through the day—a good breakfast, a nutritious afternoon snack, a reasonable and regular dinner hour, a small snack before bedtime. Your children will enjoy greater health and a more even flow of energy if they eat regularly and periodically.

Other daily events.   Adjust bath times, homework hours, play time, and practice hours (music, sports) around your established sleeping and eating times.

Something to count on.   A child who grows up with a regular schedule does not necessarily become a rigid, inflexible adult. Far from it. The results are usually greater energy and strength (from a balanced routine of food, sleep, and exercise), peace of mind (which comes from not wondering continually about what comes next or when), and a willingness to depart from the schedule periodically because he or she knows it isn't going to be the norm (actually more spontaneity, rather than less).

For you as a busy mom, a schedule means you can count on a certain rhythm being maintained, including set periods for your own relaxation. Many working mothers believe a schedule gives them a standard for determining whether life is on track and all the important bases are being covered. They feel out of control when their schedules are interrupted, even more so than when relationships are rocky, problems are looming, or family members are sick!

Schedules work for transportation systems, space flights, military missions, and sports seasons—and also for families. Think about it.

34 ● Face the Guilt

Many of today's busy moms, and especially those who work outside the home full-time, become overwhelmed by feelings of guilt. They have a nagging suspicion that they aren't doing as good a job at mothering as they should or as others are.

If that's the way you are feeling today, ask yourself

> *If I weren't working, or weren't so busy,*
> *what more would I be doing for my family?*
> *How would things be different?*

Three common answers are:

1) I'd spend more time with my children.   In reality, you probably wouldn't spend more than another hour or two a day. Many busy moms forget that their children are also busy! They're in school, at play, with friends, involved in sports, taking lessons and practicing skills, doing homework.

Rather than dwell on the amount of time you don't have with your children, make the most of the time you do have. Learn to make five-minute time intervals meaningful.

The critical point is for a mom to feel as if she is present for her children when they need her—to kiss the scraped knee, to answer the question, to hear the latest insight or discovery. If you can't be there in person, you can still be there in presence. Maintain an open-phone-line policy. Let your children know they can call you at any time, and that you want them to call. (See chapter 39.)

2) I'd make more things for my children.   Generally speaking, mothers who give this answer are thinking in terms of meals. They feel guilty for taking short-cuts on meal preparation. Not all fast foods are bad foods. Many of the meals our fore-mothers took hours to prepare didn't have as much nutritional value or taste as good as things we can zap in the microwave or boil in a bag. If you feel a need to boost the nutritional level of your family's meals, you can. It takes a few minutes of planning each week and a little adjustment to your schedule. (See chapter 10.)

Some mothers feel that if they didn't work or weren't so busy they could sew clothes, make handmade crafts as gifts, knit sweaters, and so forth for their children. Keep in mind that this may be *your* heart's desire, but your children aren't likely to know the difference. Your children will actually appreciate hand-made things more when they are adults, which is when you'll have more time to make them!

3) I'd have more energy and a better temperament.   In other words, I'd be a better person and therefore a better mom. You do have the authority to determine your moods and to take steps to reduce the amount of stress in your life.

If something is robbing you of your inner peace, or if you are always feeling on the brink of utter exhaustion, declare a "sick day" and curl up with your own thoughts. Think through what it is that you might change and how

Questions to Think About

1. Am I doing things *with* my family members or *for* them?
   What might I do *with* them?

2. Am I truly willing to let family members help with household chores—without interference or criticism?
   What chores can I delegate?

3. How flexible am I about my schedule or my agenda?
   How I might I be more flexible?

4. What rewards have I set aside for my life?
   Am I giving myself those rewards?

5. What household jobs might I pay to have done?
   If I can't afford to pay to have some of the work done, what might need to be done less often or not at all?

6. How much time am I willing to give myself on a weekly basis?
   What keeps me from giving myself this time?

7. Am I willing to put some of my goals on hold temporarily?
   Which ones?
   When might I be able to pursue those goals?

you might reorder your schedule or adjust the way you do things.

Focus on what you do give.   Busy moms have some valuable things to offer their children, apart from material well-being. Busy moms tend to see more of the world. They travel more, meet more people, encounter more information, learn more skills. Share what you see, do, and learn with your children.

Busy moms tend to be more organized because they have to be more organized. Discipline and a good work ethic are valuable traits you are modeling before your children. Talk about the importance of work with them.

Avoid comparisons with others.   They aren't healthy or helpful to you or to your children. When you begin to compare yourself with others, stop yourself mid-thought. If your children start to compare you to someone else's mom, let them know that you are you. Each life and each family is unique.

Move beyond guilt to do the best you can do. And trust the rest to the Lord.

35 🕐 Exercise with Your Child

Most busy moms know that one of the best ways to reduce stress is to exercise. What some fail to recognize is that exercise can be a fun *family* activity!

Instead of going to the health club by yourself to sweat with other adults, try doing some of the following activities with your family:

- Go bicycle riding.

- Go roller skating or ice skating.

- Take a walk around the neighborhood.

- Turn on the exercise video and do calisthenics. Or put on a dance video and teach your children the old steps, or let them teach you the new ones!

- Put on your bathing suits and go to the pool.

Use this time together to talk and to laugh. Don't compete with your children—have fun as you perspire.

Adjust your pace to accommodate your children, or mix and match activities. For example, you may need to jog while your children ride bikes. Or you may need to put the toddler in a cart that you push while you jog or pull while you cycle.

You and your children will benefit from family exercise

times—physically and relationally. Studies show repeatedly that today's children are too sedentary. They need more physical exercise.

Exercising together alleviates stress and creates a shared activity. You'll find that after exercising with your children, you actually will have more energy in the evening hours.

36 🕐 Food and Beverage Control

A busy mom can save hours of cleaning and stain-removal time, and a great deal of anxiety and dismay, if she adopts these five simple rules:

1) No food or beverages outside the kitchen and dining areas of the house. And that means *no* food or beverages, apart from water, which you may allow to be consumed in all rooms that have a faucet.

2) You must sit down while you eat. Children—especially young children—have greater control over their food and beverages if they eat and drink while sitting down. It's even difficult for adults to carry food and eat it at the same time!

Furthermore, children (as well as adults) tend to snack less frequently and to eat less of a snack food, if eating is limited to sitting down at a table.

3) Nobody may leave the table until they are properly excused. This rule allows you to make certain that your children aren't popping up from the table several times during a meal with food in their hands, loose food on their clothing, or sticky fingers.

4) Use napkins. Teach your children to use a napkin. Sometimes two napkins are better than one, especially if one is used as a bib, or the fried chicken and buttered corn on the cob are being eaten by hand.

5) Wash your hands as soon as you leave the table.   Insist that your children wash their hands and faces as soon as they leave the table.

In keeping these food and beverage rules, you automatically avoid

- The frustrating task of cleaning (or trying to clean) spills on carpets and upholstered furniture.

- Wasted food. Snack foods that end up under beds, behind desks, or wedged into the sofa tend to spoil, rot, or grow stale.

- An endless round of picking up dirty dishes and glasses all over the house.

- Bugs that are attracted to crumbs and spilled drinks.

Your children learn a basic eating etiquette that translates to other settings and will carry over into adulthood.

37 ◯ Acceptable Standards

Perfection isn't possible for any mom or any family. Set acceptable standards for yourself and others, and recognize at the outset that those standards are going to be less than perfect.

Face these facts:

You wouldn't be a perfect mother even if you were home all day, had a full-time maid, and got twelve hours of sleep at night.

You wouldn't be a perfect boss or employee if you didn't have children.

You wouldn't be the perfect woman if you didn't have family or job or outside-the-home obligations.

The house doesn't need to be spotless. It should have a sense of order and be cleaned on a regular basis.

The children don't need to be flawless in their appearance. Even if they look like catalog models when they leave your front door, they'll come home looking a little ragged at the day's end (if you allow them to be normal kids). They do need to be bathed at least once a day, have their hair brushed daily, and have clean clothes.

You don't need to cook made-from-scratch meals that win blue ribbons at the fair. Your children probably don't like food that is complicated anyway. Fix simple, nutritious meals, with as many fresh ingredients as possible.

Your children won't win every competition they enter or

score at the top of every test. They'll have their share of wins and their share of failures. Applaud the wins, comfort the failures, and encourage your children always to give their best effort.

Cut yourself a little slack and aim a little lower than perfection. Do your best and let your best be sufficient. With a more relaxed attitude, you'll probably surprise yourself and exceed your own acceptable standards! And your children will relax and enjoy more success in life, too!

38 • Let Your Children Help

Don't "wait" on your family. If you do, you'll soon feel as if you are doing all the work and receiving far less appreciation than you deserve. You'll start resenting others in your family, and if you don't stem the trend, you'll soon feel bitter and angry. Ultimately, you'll have no desire to do *anything* for your family.

Back up.

There's a simple solution. Let your children (and spouse) help out with just about everything.

Even toddlers can learn ways to help, and they *want* to. Children like to feel they are a part of the action, and that they are allowed to do what the big kids do or what Mom and Dad do.

Working together creates a sense of responsibility in a relatively pain-free way.

Adopt this simple rule of thumb:

> *Do more "with" your children,*
> *and less "for" them.*

Let your children:

- Help you strip the beds on sheet-washing day and remake the beds with fresh sheets.

- Help you fix meals or set the table.

- Help you fold laundry.

- Help you clean house.

- Help you find all of the items on your shopping list.

- Help you rake the leaves, weed the garden, and clean up the yard.

Don't be a "super mom" with lazy children. Work together. And then play together. Everybody will benefit.

39 Phone Power

Perhaps no tool benefits a busy mom more than a telephone. Here are eight tips for maximizing your phone potential:

1) Cellular. With a cellular phone you can call the children's day-care center when you are tied up in traffic or check in with your children during the day without tying up a line at work.

2) Anytime. Let your children know they can call you anytime. At the same time, encourage them not to abuse this privilege. They won't if you instill a practice of . . .

3) One-minute calls. Six or eight one-minute calls in a day can be more effective than one eight-minute call. Each call should have just one focal point—a question, a bit of information, a decision, a request, a piece of exciting news.

Depending on your work situation, you may need to ask your children to phone only during certain hours. Keep in mind, however, that if you have a cellular phone, you need not ask anyone else to answer a call from your children on your behalf.

4) Call in advance.   Call before you go. And if possible, call instead of going.

Make sure the store has what you are looking for, in the size, style, or model you want before you go to look at it. Confirm an appointment before you leave the house. Get information or resolve problems (such as getting estimates on repairs or correcting invoice errors) over the phone.

5) Accessibility.   If you have teenagers in the house, consider investing in a second line or the phone company's call-waiting service.

6) The number where you can be reached.   If you are out of town, leave the number where you can be reached (including area code) with your family. If you are at a friend's home, a meeting place, or anywhere other than where your children think you are, phone home and let them know where you can be reached.

7) Messages.   Teach your children how to answer the phone clearly and politely and how to take messages. If they are too young to write, they can learn to say, "Please call back and I'll let the machine answer the phone." Teach children who can write how to take an accurate message.

8) Answering machines.   Invest in one. If your children go any place other than where you think they are going, they should be instructed to call home. If you aren't there, they should leave a message telling you where they are, the phone number where they can be reached, and when they are coming home.

Some machines provide for multiple outgoing messages, so your child can phone in, give his or her own code, and get a personalized message from you.

A telephone is *the* vital tool for today's busy moms. Learn to make the most of one in communicating with your own children.

40 🕐 Label Garments

Busy moms do not need the aggravation of lost garments, yet the day invariably arrives when your little one comes home without his or her sweater, coat, mittens (or mitten), hat, or scarf.

A slight variation on the theme of lost garments is the situation in which your child arrives home with another child's clothes. (This often happens after sleep-overs, camping trips, or a week at sleep-away camp.)

To resolve these minor crisis moments, a busy mom can label her child's garments.

In most cases, the child's name (even first initial and last name) can be written with an indelible fabric-appropriate marking pen—the kind used by dry cleaning establishments. You can mark garments on an inside waistband, inside the back of the neckline for garments with a collar, or on a pants pocket. Don't forget to mark shoes, too, and belts.

You may also write your child's name on a washing-instructions tag in the garment or use iron-on labels personalized for your child.

Avoiding mix-ups. Sometimes the mix-up of garments takes place in your own home, especially if you have children close to the same size. Again, writing your children's names in their garments avoids confusion.

Helping match-ups. When it comes to socks, try making a couple of small stitches with a brightly colored (contrasting) thread at the toe of each sock in a pair. Use a different color for each pair of socks. You'll find that matching socks is a breeze at laundry time—something even a child can help do under the guise of a matching game.

Other items. Mark your children's school supplies (such as binders and notebooks), rackets or other sporting gear, lunch boxes, and camping equipment.

If you want to see the item again after it leaves your house with your child, label it!

41 ● Mess Control

Busy mothers need to become experts at mess control. Adopt this simple rule:

Choose the least-messy option whenever possible.

For example: If your children are making invitations, place cards, or personally designed notepaper, have them use colorfully designed stickers or colored markers instead of glitter and glue.

If your children want to serve a snack to their friends, hand-sized cookies produce less mess than cake and ice cream.

If you have your choice between offering your children chocolates that will melt in their hands, a soft-serve ice-cream cone, or a banana, choose the banana!

Wrappers. Teach your children how to use wrappers as "holders" for messy items, such as napkins around ice-cream cones, candy bar wrappers kept around candy bars, hamburger wraps kept around the bottom half of hamburgers.

Straws. Provide straws for drinks with ice.

Grubbies. Have several old garments designated as "grubbies" for your children to wear when they're helping you with messy chores.

Art smocks. Young artists need smocks or washable oversized shirts that are kept exclusively for art projects.

Newspaper mats. If your children are embarking on a craft project, put down a table-protector of newspaper. Sometimes the paper needs to go on the table and the floor beneath it.

A coating of protection. Scotch Guard your furniture. Waterproof your children's shoes.

Doormats. Insist that your children wipe their shoes on doormats that you have placed outside each entrance. If you live in an area with lots of rain and snow, ask your children to remove their boots or shoes on the back porch before they come into the main part of the house.

Washability. Moms make countless decisions each year about items that go into their homes, from appliances to furniture to toys. Ask yourself, How easy is it to clean? as you weigh your purchasing decisions. The lovely velvet pillows, the soft leather chair, and the pale blue carpeting may be your first choices. Before you buy, however, remind yourself that maintaining the appearance of such items is inversely related to the age of your children! Look for washability, durability, and flexibility.

42 ⏱ Child-Friendly Employment

Even though the job market is tight in many areas of our nation, you do have some flexibility in determining where you will work. As much as possible, associate yourself with employers and colleagues who are sympathetic to the fact that you have children.

At the time you interview. You should be on the alert for "child tolerance" as you interview for a new position and each time you are approached about advancement or promotion. Listen closely to what you are asked at the time of your interview. Be bold in asking questions in the following areas:

Overtime expectations. Many employers expect their employees (especially those who are bright and perceived to be upwardly mobile within a company) to work more than forty hours a week. Nothing may be stated in writing, but the expectation is there, nonetheless. Try to get a feel for how much time you will *really* need to spend at the job.

Flexibility. How flexible is your job situation? Can you adjust your hours—come in a half hour earlier in order to leave a half hour earlier? Can you work through lunch two days in a row in order to take off two hours on a

Friday afternoon to see your child's school play? Can you take a late lunch in order to pick up your kindergartner from school?

Can you transfer from one job responsibility to another for a period of time—perhaps for a less demanding work load or to work with others who are more sympathetic to your position as a mother?

A few companies allow persons to "share" jobs—each working half days to fill a position. This option works especially well for women who are returning to work after giving birth, women who anticipate career advancement in future years but who don't presently have the time to devote to "climbing the ladder," and women who desire a greater challenge than that offered by most part-time positions. (In some cases, full health care and retirement benefits are awarded to both persons who share a job. See what you might negotiate!)

Child provisions.   Does your company offer child-care? After-school recreational facilities?

Travel.   Are you expected to travel in your position? If so, how frequently?

Weigh your options carefully.   In considering your work commitments, ask yourself two questions:

1) Can I?   Is it physically possible for you to do what the company or organization requires of you?

2) Do I want to?   You may be able to do a job, but are you willing to make the trade-offs required?

Volunteers. Women who volunteer their time to church or community groups also should ask themselves these questions. Weigh the opportunity against the responsibility and commitment required of you and how this affects your family.

43 ● Make Lists

One of the best habits a busy mom can acquire is making lists.

Running shopping lists. Look at your family shopping needs a month at a time. You know August 1 that the children will be going back to school at the end of the month. Make a list of things they are going to need. Carry the list with you in your calendar. Pick up items as you see them in the course of your regular shopping.

Birthdays, anniversaries, and special events such as weddings and graduations are possible to anticipate a month in advance. Give yourself some lead time in purchasing, sending, or budgeting.

Grocery lists, on the other hand, are likely to be weekly lists. Keep a running list posted in a place where every person in your family can add to it.

If you are looking for a particular item for your home, keep information about that item with you in your calendar, such as the dimensions of the space in your home for the item, the price you were quoted at Store X, and the features you want or need.

Survey your children's clothing every few months and make notes about items they will need in the near future.

Watch for sales. (Be sure to write down sizes for each family member.)

Keep a running Christmas shopping list, too. Buy gifts throughout the year as you find items that are appropriate to those on your gift-giving list.

Carry running lists with you at all times so you can add to them at any time.

Daily lists. Make a list each day of things to do. Before leaving work, write a list of things to do tomorrow. Consult your calendar as you make your daily list. You'll probably sleep better since you no longer have to remember the events on tomorrow's agenda through the night hours.

Other lists. You may want to keep lists of

- People to call.

- Notes to write.

- Information to get.

Nothing is too big, too small, or too strange to put on a list. After all, it's your list, not an item for public consumption. Put anything down on a list that you want to make sure you remember to do.

A list frees up brain power for other things. Your mind no longer needs to rehearse information and obligations. The list serves as your memory, and you are free to think of other things. You may very well find, as many list makers do, that you can listen to others with greater concentration, fidget less, and experience greater inner calm. At work, you may find you can focus your ideas and concentrate more effectively.

Lists give your day structure and provide a sense of accomplishment as you mark things *off* the list.

The busier you are, the more you need lists!

44 ● Get the Help You Need

Nobody can do it all. Whenever possible, delegate. Or hire. Or ask.

You may need to negotiate the division of responsibilities in your home. Unfortunately, many women wait until they are at their emotional and sometimes physical breaking point before they insist that others help carry the load (or live with the consequences of certain things not being done). Try to anticipate ahead of tears, anger, and exhaustion what you need in the way of help. Make a comprehensive list of the things you do in a week that benefit the entire family, and indicate next to each task how long it takes you to do that task.

Share your list with your spouse. Your husband may not have a clue that you are doing so many things for the family or that they take so long to do. If you turn over an area of home-care responsibility to him, let him do the job without interference. (See chapter 37.) Don't redo what he does. Don't undo it. Don't nag him about it. You may want to ask if he would like to have a chore list similar to the one you have for the children as a reminder of the things he has agreed to do on a daily or weekly basis. Sometimes a list helps build a habit. (You might also point out that a list for both of you as parents would be a good example to set for the children.)

Both of you may decide that certain chores need to be

hired out. Two-job families usually need double the budget for transportation and fuel, career clothes, lunches out, and so forth. Part of the cost of earning a living should include help with those chores that one of you would tend to do if you were home all day.

Keep in mind that volunteer work also carries with it a cost in terms of time.

45 ● Get the Help Your Children Need

Just as you can't *do* all of the physical tasks required to keep a family "operational," you can't *be* everything to your children.

Your children not only need teachers for some subjects and coaches for others. They need:

Fans. Let your children develop a close relationship with an aunt or uncle, grandparents, a godparent, or a family friend who will take a special interest in their development and be quick to applaud their successes.

Big Brother, Big Sister, and adoptive grandparent programs are options you might consider.

Counsel. Sometimes good counsel may come from a coach or Sunday school teacher. Sometimes it may need to come from a professional counselor. If your children are struggling emotionally as the result of a divorce, abuse, or some type of crisis event, seek help for them. If you suspect they are experimenting with drugs, or if they exhibit major changes in mood, attitude, or behavior, get help. It's not an admission of poor parenting on your part to seek a psychologist or family counselor. It's a sign of good mothering!

If your children show signs of disruptive behavior at school, listen closely to what their teachers say and suggest. Don't become defensive or confrontational. Your children's teachers are on your side; be on theirs.

Tutors.   Don't let your children struggle with a particular school subject. Get a tutor. Sometimes local college students are available to provide tutoring for little or no cost.

Mentors.   If your children show a particular aptitude or skill for music or some other creative or artistic field, or, if they show exceptional physical ability, seek the advice of a professional in that field. What lessons might benefit them, or help them to realize their maximum potential? Provide those lessons as best you can.

Socialization.   Sometimes children need to learn how to fit in or to feel comfortable around other people. Dance classes, etiquette courses, or long talks with a trusted adult can help children learn what to do, how to act, what to wear, or how to talk. Seek older and wiser friends for your children.

Allies.   Your children need persons who will be personally supportive, instructive, and loving. If at any time you suspect that persons you *thought* were allies are abusive or manipulative, end the association immediately. Believe your children when they tell you what is happening or how they are feeling.

46 🕐 Family Meetings

Periodically, sit down with your family and check signals.

Structure the event as a meeting, just as you might experience a meeting at work. That approach lowers the emotional temperature of the encounter, which usually makes for a more productive time of decision-making and problem-solving.

Announce the time and place of the meeting several days in advance. Limit the time to an hour.

Solicit agenda items. Each family member should be allowed to introduce topics of concern. Prepare a written agenda so you can see how much needs to be covered during the meeting.

Call the meeting to order. Have someone record the decisions that are made. Move through the agenda in a step-by-step manner.

Even though you are conducting this family discussion in a businesslike manner, you'll want to leave room for an objective discussion of feelings. Teach your children how to state their feelings without yelling, crying, withdrawing, or acting out.

You'll probably want to include these general areas of discussion as a part of your meeting:

The family calendar. Go over your calendar for

the next few weeks. Make certain you each *need* to do everything you are scheduled to do. Talk about various events and time commitments. Anticipate what may need to be done in advance of certain events. Above all,

> *Ask how other family members are feeling*
> *about their present time obligations*
> *and the overall pace of the family.*

Families sometimes get so caught up in a frantic series of meetings, games, or obligations, that they hardly speak to one another or have time truly to be together. If that's the conclusion you reach as a family, make adjustments.

Personal difficulties and challenges. Face

up to specific difficulties a particular family member may be experiencing. For example, if your teenage daughter is struggling to learn her lines for the school play, this is a time to give her an extra dose of cooperation, understanding, and quiet time. If your son is trying out for the tennis team, he may want to spend more time at the practice court. How might you adjust the family routine?

Keep in mind that most of these personal crises and challenges are short-term. You may need to bend in the direction of one family member for a few days, but he or she will likely need to bend in your direction in the future.

Family problems or challenges. If your chil-

dren are at each other's throats continually, get to the bottom of the squabble and decide what action to take.

If you or your spouse are scheduled to be away for a

few days, use the family meeting to discuss who is going to help out with your responsibilities—how and when.

Decisions.   End the family meeting by reviewing the list of decisions you have reached. You may want to post a new rule or policy on the family bulletin board for a few days to keep it a "live thought" in the minds of all family members.

Periodic meetings help keep a family on track. Don't wait for a problem to come to a full boil or a trend to build into a crisis.

End your meeting with handshakes or hugs all around.

47 🕐 Mom's Night Out

Moms need an occasional block of time to call their own each week.

Some busy moms may take advantage of a mother's day out program offered by a neighborhood church or child-care center. These programs give busy moms an entire morning or afternoon each week to be by themselves.

Moms who work full-time, however, will probably have to find this time during an evening or on the weekend. Hire a baby-sitter if you need to. Trade off "going out" times with friends. Take the children to a child-care center that provides baby-sitting services by the hour. Do what you need to do to get some time alone and away. (If you are divorced and your husband has weekly visitation times, you may be able to use one of these times as your morning, afternoon, or night out.)

The difference between a time-out (chapter 5) and "going out" is two-fold:

1) Going-out time needs to be at least two to three consecutive hours. Anything less than that isn't a true break.

2) Going-out time needs to be spent *away* from the house.

Use this time to nurture yourself. Do something that gives you pleasure, and don't feel guilty about it.

Three hours is less than 2 percent of the total hours in a week. Consider it time invested in yourself, to make yourself a more loving, interesting, fun-to-be-with mom. Here are some suggested going-out activities:

- Go shopping at leisure.

- Have lunch or dinner with a friend or friends.

- Go to a movie, a lecture, a concert, a recital, or a play.

- Have your hair or nails done.

- Get a massage.

- Take a long walk or bicycle ride or even a drive through the countryside.

Choose activities that inspire you, calm you, build you up, and truly give you a break from your obligations and routine. You'll probably find you have more emotional reserve and physical energy to face the pressures of the other 165 hours a week.

Once a month. If you can't fathom taking two to three hours a week for yourself, at least schedule this time for yourself every two weeks, or at the minimum, once a month. Consider it burn-out prevention!

48 🕐 Play Groups

Cultivate a group of friends with whom your children can play on a regular and structured basis.

You can put together this circle of friends in your immediate neighborhood. If there aren't any youngsters in your neighborhood who are the same ages as your children, try forming a play group of your children's friends from church or school.

Here's how a play group works.

At a designated time each week the children gather with the sole purpose of playing together. Parents rotate supervision of the play group so that no one parent is responsible for more than one play period a month.

Aim at a play group size of between six and ten children. That is enough children for some forms of team play, yet the group won't be totally unmanageable. You may need to designate two parents as "supervisors," depending on the size of the group.

The play group may or may not meet at one of the homes. In the summer go to the community pool. The "parent-in-charge" acts as a second lifeguard to watch the children. In winter, the "playground" can be the local ice-skating rink. In the fall and spring months, the children can play at a local park. There's no wear and tear on any one home that way. And the children enjoy the change of venue!

Supervising parents may not need to watch the children all that closely, or get involved in the play. For example at the ice-skating rink, the parent-in-charge can sit on the sidelines and write notes, crochet, read, or balance the checkbook. The children know, however, that an adult is in "residence" and available for consultation, applause, or emergencies.

Each parent is responsible for bringing his or her children to the designated place at a designated time, for picking them up (again, on time), and for providing any money their children might need for snacks or admission.

Play groups are a no-expense approach to babysitting. Supervising parents enjoy the opportunity to watch their own children interact with others. Parents who have the week off enjoy the hours to pursue their own activities.

49 ① State "The Plan" Beforehand

Children behave better and life goes more smoothly if everyone in the family knows what to expect.

School. Tour the school with your children before the first day of classes. If possible, introduce each child to his or her teacher before classes begin.

The same goes for church school classes. Before the first class, walk your children through the process of going to a class and of finding you afterward. Let them get a feel for where they will be and where you will be. Children are often reluctant to leave their parents at a classroom door because they have no idea where their parents are going to be or how they can find them if they need them.

Shopping. Before entering a store, state clearly what it is you are going to buy and what you aren't going to buy. Have the candy or toy issue settled before going in the store.

Visits to relatives and friends. Before stopping to visit relatives or friends, remind your children who it is you are going to visit. If they have never met these people, tell them a little about who the people are, their work, their relationship to your family, and special accomplishments they may have. Suggest questions to ask, and let your children know what you expect them to "do" during the visit. Don't say, Behave yourself. Tell them *how* to behave, and define what they will be allowed to do to entertain themselves. (This may be a time when your children can use their activity bags. See chapter 18.) Finally, give your children an idea about how long a visit you are planning.

Vacations.   Get a map and show your children where you are going. Describe a little about the process of traveling that lies ahead. Let them know how long (in terms of time, not miles) you will be traveling. Mention things to look for along the way, and don't exaggerate how much fun the trip is going to be. Think in terms of adventure or experience rather than fun. Your children's idea of fun may be far different from yours!

Camp.   If possible, visit your children's sleep-away camp before they go. Drive around the facilities. Peek inside the cabins or tents. Help your children get a feel for what life will be like there, so they will be more confident about going away for a week or two.

New experiences.   It may be your child's first airplane flight, first concert, first time to sleep over at a friend's house, or first visit to the big-league ball park. Adults tend to forget that each of these "firsts" for children has a little bit of trauma attached to it. Anticipate possible questions your children may have, and talk about what appropriate behavior will be in the new situation. Give them information about what to do in a possible emergency, for example, if you get separated. Put yourself in your children's shoes as best you can. What is it that might worry you about the upcoming new experience? (For some children, it's just knowing where the bathrooms will be. For others, it's how to make friends.)

By stating the plan to your children, you will be setting them up for success. In the long run, they will be more confident about facing new challenges.

50 ● Take a Vacation Day with Your Children

How many vacation days do you have a year? If you're employed full-time, you probably have at least a week's worth. Consider taking at least two or three of those days to spend as one-day "mini-vacations" with your children.

- Go to the zoo together.

- Go fishing.

- Take in a matinee, with lunch and a little shopping beforehand.

- Drive to the beach, or to the mountains, or to the country to see the farms in spring or autumn.

- Pack a picnic and go to the park.

- Spend a day Christmas shopping and seeing the lights.

Your children are likely to have several days during the year that are designated by their school as teacher days or holiday breaks. One of those days may be your best day for a mini-vacation.

Let your children help decide what to do. Keep the day free-form and casual. Allow for detours and spontaneous changes in your plan. Explore the world together. Choose to be amused at life.

These vacation days can be wonderful experiences for you and your children. For you, it's a true break from work. For your children, it's a time to feel special; a memory in the making.

51 ● Develop a Family Support Group

A healthy and helpful thing you can do for your family as a busy mom, is to forge friendships with other families who have children the same age as yours.

Do things as "clusters of families." You'll develop a support community for yourself and your children that will be invaluable in times of crisis, in coping with peer pressure problems, and in teaching your children how to be friends.

This may be a neighborhood group, a cluster of families at church, or a group of families that get to know one another through Little League, school band activities, or scouting.

You may want to have a monthly pot-luck dinner together. Rotate responsibilities for: 1) providing house, dishes, silverware, and main dish, 2) vegetable side dish, 3) salad, 4) bread and beverage, and 5) dessert. That way, no one family is burdened more than any other.

Share meals outside to allow the children plenty of room to play, or meet for picnics at a park. Agree on times to begin and end the evening.

Vacations. Families may want to take trips together, such as camping, houseboating, or touring. Or go to a special out-of-town event together (to a ball game, an amusement park, or a concert in a nearby city).

Compatibility. Give yourself time to develop a group such as this. Don't assume that the first families with whom you share activities or pot-lucks are going to be ones you want to see forever. Seek families with whom you share values. Such a community of friends will be of great support to you as you attempt to build strong values in your children.

52 🕐 Pray for Your Children

No matter how busy you are, make the time, take the time, set aside the time to pray for your children.

Pray for each child daily. State his or her individual needs to the Lord. Pray for the things that you desire to see develop within your children as traits—faithfulness, honesty, steadfastness, an ability to communicate openly and honestly. Pray for their friendships and their ability to make friends, their ability to learn and to remember, their ability to do their best at each task they undertake. Pray for their future—their spouses, their choices about a career, their opportunities to give of themselves to the world.

Is your child experiencing a difficulty, or going through a "hard" growth stage? Ask the Lord to give you compassion, extra patience, and wisdom about how to help your child through this time.

You can pray for your children as you drive to work, as you take breaks at work, as you drive home. Assure them that you will be praying for them as they take difficult tests, try out for teams, or face new challenges.

Pray with ***your children.*** Gather your children around you and say a prayer together before they leave for school and you leave for work.

Pray with your children at bedtime. Encourage them to pray, too. You'll discover a depth to your children in times of prayer that you might easily overlook by racing through a day's routine.

Let your children join you in prayer. As you see needs, pray together as a family about them. Let your children join with you in praying for the homeless persons they see along the streets of your city, the victims of catastrophes they see on the news, the sick family member you all love, the neighbor who is having surgery, the child they know whose parents are going through a divorce. You will build a strong bond as a family by praying for others.

Repentance and forgiveness. Are you feeling guilty about something you feel you aren't doing or being as a mom? Ask the Lord to show you what to do and how and when to do it. Have you had miscommunication or an argument with your children? Ask their forgiveness and, together, ask the Lord to help you to be more loving and understanding of one another. Are you feeling resentment about all of the things you must do as a mother? Are you feeling overwhelmed? Talk to the Lord about it, and ask for His help.

The Bible tells us that "love will cover a multitude of sins" (1 Peter 4:8). Prayer is the language that breeds love.